Bible-Teaching
FINGER PLAYS

Bible-Teaching FINGER PLAYS

by
Marian White

BAKER BOOK HOUSE, Grand Rapids, Michigan

Illustrations by Robert Winter

Formerly published under the titles, *Through the Bible with Finger Plays,* ᶜ1965 by Marian White, and *More Bible Finger Plays,* ᶜ1974 by Baker Book House.

Combined edition issued 1977 by Baker Book House

ISBN: 0-8010-9592-1

Fourth printing, January 1984

PHOTOLITHOPRINTED BY CUSHING - MALLOY, INC.
ANN ARBOR, MICHIGAN, UNITED STATES OF AMERICA

HOW TO USE THIS BOOK

PURPOSE OF THIS BOOK

The aim of this book is to supply the teacher of preschool children with finger plays for the Bible stories that all small children love. The material covers both testaments.

WHAT ARE FINGER PLAYS?

Finger plays are simple rhymes coupled with finger actions. Instead of singing the rhyme, the child acts out the finger play—one of his favorite pastimes.

The history of finger plays is a long one for they have been well known in China alone for hundreds of years. Like nursery rhymes, they were a natural outgrowth of the child's love to play with his hands and to try to repeat his mother's words.

PURPOSE OF FINGER PLAYS

Finger plays have a twofold purpose: (1) to entertain and (2) to teach through play.

All children delight in doing finger plays and the plays are an excellent device for recapturing the attention of restless children.

Through finger plays the teacher introduces the child to a whole new world of fascinating people and ideas, in this case, the small child's world of the Bible. The child acts out what he has learned in the Bible story. At the same time, he acquires a vocabulary of Biblical words that would be difficult to teach him by any other method. (For the very young child, the teacher may need to teach only part of the finger play.)

CONTENTS

SECTION ONE
FINGER PLAYS ABOUT THE BIBLE AS A BOOK

SECTION ONE

FINGER PLAYS ABOUT THE BIBLE AS A BOOK

THE ONE BOOK

There is one God.   *(hold up index finger—right hand)*
He has one Book.   *(hold up index finger—left hand)*
This Book He gave to us.   *(make book with hands)*
It tells the way   *(hold up index finger—left hand)*
To go to God.   *(point heavenward)*
The way? Jesus!   *(spread hands)*

THE BIBLE HAS TWO PARTS

The Bible has two parts: *(hold up index fingers only)*
The Old Testament   *(open all fingers—right hand)*
And the New.   *(open all fingers—left hand)*
Put the parts together,   *(let thumbs touch)*
It's God's book for me   *(nod head)*
And for you.   *(hold out book)*

IN ALL THE WORLD

In all the world—   *(make circle with arms)*
Though you look and look—   *(put hands to eyes, look back
                                       and forth)*
You will never find   *(shake head)*
Another book
LIKE THE BIBLE!   *(make book with hands)*

STOP AND GO

Stop! says the Bible   *(hand signal for* stop)
When I am bad.
Go! says the Bible   *(hand signal for* go)
When I am good.
This way I can know   *(nod head)*
When to *stop!* when to *go!*   *(repeat signals)*

13

THE BIBLE

This is the Bible;   *(make book)*

Open it wide,   *(open book)*
Tell me the story   *(pretend to read)*
*Of Jesus inside.

    *Substitute other names

GOD'S BOOK AND I

God gave me eyes,   *(point to eyes)*
God gave me ears,   *(touch ears)*
God gave me a mouth too.   *(touch lips)*
I see his book,   *(make book)*
I hear his book,   *(cup ears)*
Then I tell it to you!   *(point to other children)*

JIMMY'S BIBLE

Jimmy has a nice Bible,   *(make book)*
It is his favorite book;
Jimmy goes to Bible class,   *(walk where you stand)*
Does he take his Bible? Look! *(make book; tuck under arm)*

MY BIBLE

Here is my Bible,	*(make book)*
And this I know:	*(nod head)*
Every day	
I love it so!	*(hug book)*

I PICK UP MY BIBLE

I pick up my Bible,	*(pick up book)*
I walk along,	*(walk where you stand)*
To the place of worship	
Where I belong.	*(stop walking)*

GOD GAVE US THE BIBLE

God gave us the Bible,	*(point right hand to others;*
But that's not all.	*left hand to self)*
He gave us: hands to hold it,	*(tuck book under arm)*
eyes to read it,	*(pretend to read open book)*
ears to hear it,	*(touch ears)*
heart to do it.	*(touch heart)*

OPEN AND READ IT

Open and read it.	*(pretend to read open book)*
Open and read it.	*(repeat action next three lines)*
Open and read God's Book.	
Open and read it.	
Open and read it.	
Seven days a week—Look!	*(hold up seven fingers)*

AT BIBLE STORYTIME

To hear a story

(cup hands behind ears)

From God's Holy Book

(make book)

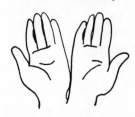

I close my mouth—

(touch mouth)

Just listen and look.

(touch ears and eyes)

I WILL NEVER KNOW

If I take the Bible,   *(hold open book)*
Then close it up tight,   *(close book)*
I will never know   *(shake head)*
How to do what's right!   *(spread hands helplessly)*

TAKE CARE OF GOD'S BOOK

God has one Book,   *(hold up one finger)*
The Holy Bible.   *(make book)*
I love it every bit.
I hold it so—   *(open hands carefully)*
I dust it so—   *(close book and dust with one hand)*
I take good care of it.

COUNT WITH ME

ONE for the Bible;   *(hold up index finger—right hand)*
TWO for my ears.   *(cup left ear with left hand)*
I WILL STUDY THE BIBLE *(raise right hand for oath)*
Year after year!

I CAN SPELL

J-E-S-U-S spells Jesus   *(hold up five fingers)*
The *name* of God's Son.
B-I-B-L-E spells Bible,
The *book* about God's Son.

I TELL ABOUT JESUS

The Bible tells me about Jesus; *(make book)*
Then I tell *you*.   *(point to others)*
Now *you* tell someone about
    Jesus
And make *him* happy too.   *(clasp hands)*

GRANDMOTHER'S GLASSES

These are grandmother's
    glasses.   *(circle each eye with fingers)*
This is grandmother's cap.   *(interlock fingers over head)*
She reads the Bible to me.   *(make book)*
While I sit in her lap.

LITTLE BIBLE

Little Bible,   *(make book; address it)*
Book divine;
I'm very glad   *(raise book proudly)*
You are mine.   *(hug book)*

18

SECTION TWO
OLD TESTAMENT FINGER PLAYS

SECTION TWO

OLD TESTAMENT FINGER PLAYS

DAY ONE   **Genesis 1:3-5**

On day one,

*(hold up index finger —
left hand)*

God made the light;

(make sweep with right hand)

Then there was
Both day and night.

*(hold out right hand,
then left hand)*

21

DAY TWO   Genesis 1:6-8

On day two,   *(hold up two fingers –*
                                        left hand)

God made the sky —   *(point to sky – right hand)*
Oh, so blue,
And up so high.

DAY THREE   Genesis 1:9-13

On day three,   *(hold up three fingers)*
God made the ground   *(spread hands flat)*
And the trees,   *(arms high)*
So tall and round.

DAY FOUR   Genesis 1:14-19

On day four,   *(hold up four fingers)*
God made the sun,   *(make circle with arms)*
The moon, the stars,   *(arms high; wiggle*
                                        fingers for stars)
For everyone.   *(spread arms wide)*

DAY FIVE   Genesis 1:20-23

On day five,   *(five fingers)*
God made the fish;   *(palms together in*
                                        diving position)

Then the birds —
To fly — swish!   *(flap arms fast)*

DAY SIX   Genesis 1:24-31

On day six,   *(six fingers)*
God made to walk
Animals;   *(walk fingers along arm)*
Then man to talk.   *(touch mouth)*

DAY SEVEN Genesis 2:2–3

By day seven,   *(hold up seven fingers)*
God was done.   *(spread hands flat)*
And He stopped work   *(fold hands)*
Up in heaven.   *(point up)*

WHOSE NAME IS FIRST? Genesis 1:1

Whose name comes first?   *(hold up closed book)*
In all the Bible   *(hold up one finger)*
The one Holy Book?
The name of God   *(point up)*
In the *first* verse.   *(point at closed book)*
Now *you* come and look.   *(open book and extend to class)*

LOOK UP! Genesis 1:1

Look up, up!   *(point to sky)*
See the sky?
Look down, down!   *(point to ground)*
See the ground?
God made more—   *(nod head)*
Turn around!   *(turn around—point with fingers)*

LET THERE BE LIGHT Genesis 1:3

First God said,   *(point up)*
"Let there be light."   *(point out)*
Did the light shine?   *(spread hands)*
Just like that!   *(snap fingers)*

DRAW A CIRCLE Genesis 1:4–5

Draw a circle.   *(draw a circle)*
Cut it this way.   *(draw vertical line in center)*
This is night.   *(point to right half of circle)*
This is day.   *(point to left half of circle)*

23

THE BIG BALL   Genesis 1:9–10

This is the earth,	*(make circle with arms)*
A big, big ball!	
Who made the earth?	*(spread hands outward in question)*
God made it all!	*(repeat first action, and look heavenward)*

GOD MAKES THINGS GROW   Genesis 1:11–12

Here are grains of corn,	*(hold out cupped hands)*
I plant them in a row.	*(pretend to plant them)*
God sends rain,	*(flutter fingers downward)*
And sunshine.	*(hold arms down stiffly for rays of sun)*
Now watch the grain grow.	*(raise hands—palms up— to show growth)*

THE PRETTY FLOWER   Genesis 1:11–12

This is a flower;	*(cup hands)*
Open it wide	*(open hands slowly)*
To show how pretty	*(tilt for all to see)*
God made it inside.	*(hold flower toward heaven)*

WHO MADE THE TREES?   Genesis 1:11–12

First, the trunk; then, the branches,	*(hold up right arm; then open fingers)*
And there you have a tall tree;	*(look up at it)*
Who made all the lovely trees?	*(spread hands to include imaginary trees)*
God did—for the birds and me!	*(point upward; outward; to self)*

GOD MADE THE BIRDS   Genesis 1:21

God made the birds	*(touch thumbs—move hands up and down for wings)*
To fly in the sky.	
We can hear them sing	
As they fly by.	*(continue flying action)*

LITTLE FLY   Genesis 1:24-31

Tell me, little fly,   *(address fly on finger)*
Who made you?
I know the answer!   *(nod head)*
God did. Now shoo!   *(flick off fly)*

THE GARDEN OF EDEN   Genesis 2:8-9

God made a garden   *(spread arms wide)*
For Adam and Eve;   *(hold up index fingers)*
It was their first home;
Till God made them leave.   *(walk fingers along arm)*

WHO NAMED THE ANIMALS?   Genesis 2:24–25

God made the animals—   *(point upwards)*

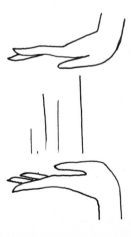

Some big—some small.   *(measure high for large animals*

25

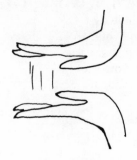

and low for smaller)

They came to Adam;

(walk first two fingers of each hand to make animals' four legs)

He named them all.

(hold up index finger)

HELLO, GARDEN   Genesis 2:8–9, 22

Hello, Garden of Eden,
Said Adam and Eve.
You are our very first home—
We do now believe.

(wave right hand; then, left)

GOOD-BYE, GARDEN   Genesis 3:23—24

Good-bye, garden,   *(wave both hands)*
Said Adam and Eve—
We hate to go,
But sin made us leave.   *(walk four fingers away)*

ONE, TWO, THREE   Genesis 3:23—24

One is for Adam,   *(hold up pointer finger—left hand)*
Two is for Eve: *(hold up second finger also)*
Three for the garden   *(hold up third finger—left hand)*
That they had to leave.   *(close three fingers tightly
                                        again)*

TWO BROTHERS   Genesis 4:1—2

A-is for Abel,   *(hold up index finger—left hand,
                                        point to it)*
B-is for brothers,   *(nod head slightly)*
C-is for Cain—   *(hold up next finger—left hand,
                                        point to it)*

Cain and Abel were brothers.   *(close fingers of right hand
                                        around two fingers of
                                        left hand)*

THE FIRST TWO BOYS   Genesis 4:1-2

Who was the first boy?   *(hold up index finger –
                                        left hand)*
Who was his brother?   *(other index finger)*
The first boy was Cain,   *(raise that finger)*
Abel was his brother.   *(raise other finger)*

WHAT DID CAIN DO?   Genesis 4:1—8

Cain and Abel   *(hold up index fingers)*
Both made offerings to God;   *(spread hands—palms up)*
But Cain's offering was bad.   *(point thumb down)*
God would not take it.   *(shake head)*
Cain killed his brother   *(let one index finger knock
                                        other down)*

Why? Because he was so mad!   *(close fist angrily)*

27

THE FIRST THREE   Genesis 4:1-2, 25

One is for Cain	*(hold up one finger)*
The first boy.	
Two is for Abel	*(hold up second finger)*
Killed by Cain.	
Three is for Seth	*(hold up third finger)*
Who took Abel's place—	
The first three sons	*(raise the three fingers)*
In the human race!	

WHY SEND THE FLOOD?   Genesis 5:5, 17

See this big ball?	*(make circle with arms)*
It is mine, you know.	*(point to self)*
When it's dirty,	
I wash it — so!	*(washing motions)*
The earth is a ball,	*(make circle)*
All blue and green;	
God sent a big flood	*(hands flat; raise slowly)*
To wash it clean.	*(admire circle)*

FOOD IN THE ARK?   Genesis 6:21-22

The people in the ark	*(hold up eight fingers)*
And the animals too,	*(closed fist plus two fingers for ears)*
Would be hungry more and more;	
So God had Noah	*(one finger high—then one low)*
Carry in much food	*(spread arms)*
Before God shut the one door.	*(close door)*

OPEN THE DOOR   Genesis 7:7-9

Here's the door of the ark—	*(hold up right hand—palm toward you)*
Open it wide.	*(turn hand away from you)*
So all the animals	*(make wide sweep away from door with left hand)*
Can go inside.	*(walk two fingers of the other hand past the door— keep repeating)*

WHO WERE IN THE ARK?   Genesis 7:13

See who were in the ark?   *(show eight fingers)*
Only a few.
But I can count them all.   *(nod)*
How about you?   *(count fingers)*

TWO BY TWO   Genesis 7:15

Here is Noah's big ark,   *(hands flat; one six inches
                                       above the other)*
Here is Noah too.   *(hold up index finger)*
Here come the animals,   *(walk fingers along arm)*
Two by two.

WHO SHUT THE DOOR?   Genesis 7:16

Noah built the ark   *(pounding)*
With one window and   *(raise index fingers in turn)*
    one door.
When the ark was done,
It was God who shut   *(clap hands once)*
    the door.

THE FLOOD   Genesis 7:17-20

The rains came down, down,   *(flutter fingers down)*
The waters went up, up,   *(raise palms slowly)*
Until the tall trees   *(arms high — fingers spread)*
Were all covered up!

THE RAVEN   Genesis 8:6–7

Open the window,   *(make square with arms)*
Let the raven go;   *(pretend to hold bird in right
                                       hand; toss it out the window)*
Till the earth is dry,   *(spread hands)*
He will fly to and fro.   *(flap arms)*

LITTLE DOVE   Genesis 8:8-9

Little dove, little dove,	*(address bird on finger)*
Fly, fly, fly,	*(toss into air)*
Help Noah see if the	
Ground is dry.	*(look downwards)*
Little dove, little dove,	*(look up to sky)*
Where are you?	
Sitting in a dry tree,	*(arm high)*
Coo, coo, coo.	*(cooing sounds)*

NOAH SAID, THANK-YOU   Genesis 8:20-21

Noah built an altar	*(pick up stones; make small pile)*
To say, Thank-you.	
I can build on altar.	*(continue action)*
How about you?	*(stop; point to others)*

THE RAINBOW   Genesis 9:13-14

Draw half a circle;	*(top half)*
Do it again.	*(repeat just below)*
See God's rainbow,	*(point to bow)*
After the rain?	

ABRAHAM, ABRAHAM   Genesis 12:1-4

Abraham, Abraham,	*(address index finger)*
Whom do you love?	
The one who calls me friend,	*(point to self)*
God up above.	*(point to heaven)*

A BIG QUESTION   Genesis 12:1

Abraham, Abraham,	*(hold up index finger; talk to it)*
Where did you go?	*(address Abraham)*
To follow God to a	*(walk two fingers into distance)*
Land I do not know.	

ABRAHAM BUILT AN ALTAR   Genesis 12:8

Up, up the mountain	*(hold arms high with fingertips touching)*
Abraham went	*(walk two fingers of left hand up right arm to shoulder)*
To build an altar	*(hold arms up with one hand flat on top of the other hand)*
And pitch his tent.	*(lower arms—make a tent with hands)*

ANOTHER BIG QUESTION   Genesis 12:8

Abraham, Abraham, Why do you stop?	*(hold up index finger—address it)*
To pray to God On the mountain top.	*(bend finger at first knuckle for bowed head)*

GOD BLESSED ABRAHAM   Genesis 13:2

God blessed Abraham	*(hold hands out as if blessing him)*
With much cattle and sheep,	*(count, in turn, fingers on left hand)*
With silver and gold,	*(count two more fingers)*
They were all his to keep.	*(close fingers of left hand in grip)*

CHOOSE!   Genesis 13:8–9

Abraham told Lot:	*(hold up index finger—right hand; then left hand)*
We must not fight,	*(shake both fingers)*
If you go to the right	*(point to right)*
I'll go to the left;	*(point to left)*
If you go the the left	*(point to left)*
I'll go to the right.	*(point to right)*

WHAT DID LOT TAKE?   Genesis 13:10–11

Lot looked this way,   *(put hand to eye—look to left)*
And saw poor land.
Lot looked that way,   *(put hand to eye—look to right)*
And saw good land.
What did Lot take?   *(spread hands)*
He took the best.   *(point to the right)*
And Abraham?   *(spread hands)*
He took the rest!   *(point to the left)*

THE NEW NAME   Genesis 17:5

Take the name Abram—   *(hold up a name plate)*
S-t-r-e-t-c-h it as you do gum;   *(stretch the name as you would
                                          a piece of gum)*
You have Abraham   *(hold up longer name plate)*
God's new name for Abram.   *(raise name higher)*

ABRAHAM'S WIFE   Genesis 17:15

Abraham had a wife   *(hold up index finger—right hand)*
Sarah was her name.   *(hold up index finger—left hand
                                          beside Abram)*
Each time he followed God,   *(move Abram to the right)*
Sarah did the same.   *(move Sarah after him—stop
                                          beside him)*

WHAT A PITY!   Genesis 18:26–32; 19:24–25

God would have saved Sodom   *(point up)*
If this many righteous   *(hold up ten fingers)*
People could have been found;   *(look around)*
But He could not find ten.   *(hold up ten fingers)*
So fire from heaven   *(flutter open hands downwards)*
Burned Sodom to the ground!   *(hold hands high and flat—drop lov*

32

LOT'S WIFE   Genesis 19:17, 26

The Lord had told Lot's family Not to look back nor halt;	*(hold up four fingers –* *right hand)*
But Lot's wife turned around to look —	*(index finger only)*
She turned into salt!	*(clap hands before* *word she)*

THE TWINS GREW UP   Genesis 25:25–28

Esau grew up	*(hang arms at sides: bring right* *arm up halfway)*
To be a hunter;	*(use left hand to aim imaginary* *bow and arrow)*
A hairy skin had he.	*(run fingers of right hand along* *left arm)*
Jacob grew up	*(bring left arm up halfway)*
To be a shepherd;	*(use right hand to grasp imaginary* *shepherd's staff)*
A s-m-o-o-t-h skin had he!	*(run fingers of left hand along* *right arm)*

JACOB'S PILLOW   Genesis 28:10–11

One night Jacob	*(hold up index finger—right hand)*
Slept outdoors With the ground for his bed.	*(hold out left hand—palm up; lay* *finger on it)*
And some big stones—	*(pretend to pick up some stones* *with both hands)*
What were they? Pillows under his head!	*(put a stone behind your head)*

JACOB'S DREAM   Genesis 28:11-14

Jacob had a dream	*(sleep head on hands)*
Of a ladder reaching high;	*(raise arms high)*
Angels were walking	*(walk fingers up and down* *on a "ladder")*
On the ladder in the sky.	

JOSEPH'S NEW COAT   Genesis 37:3

See Joseph's new coat?   *(hold up)*
How pretty it is!
He puts it on—so.   *(do so)*
He's glad it is his.

Who gave it to him?   *(touch coat)*
His grandmother? No!   *(shake head)*
Jacob, his father
Who loved him so!   *(hug coat)*

PHARAOH'S CHARIOT   Genesis 41:43

See Pharaoh's chariot?   *(hold up left hand with palm up
                                and fingers stiffly bent upward
                                for front of chariot—double up
                                right fist and hold underneath
                                left hand for wheels)*
He can stand or sit.   *(bend middle finger—right hand
                                toward you for Pharaoh)*
These are the wheels,   *(raise chariot slightly to show them)*
A fast horse pulls it!   *(make chariot move quickly across
                                in front of you)*

LITTLE BABY MOSES   Exodus 2:1-3

Moses' mother
Took a basket —   *(cup hands slightly)*
Made it like a boat;
Put Moses in it,   *(set basket down; lay
                                    baby in it)*
On the river —
There the boat did float.   *(rock hands)*

THE SURPRISE   Exodus 2:1-6

Miriam, Miriam,   *(address index finger)*
Whom did you bring
To nurse your baby
    brother?
I ran and I ran quickly,   *(move finger quickly to right)*
Till I found her —   *(hold up other index finger)*
Our very own mother!   *(move fingers back quickly)*

HURRY! HURRY!   Exodus 1:8–14

One brick,	*(count off each on left hand)*
Two bricks,	
Three bricks,	
And four.	
Then it's time	*(hold both hands—palms up—as if gripping a brick)*
To make some more!	
Hurry, hurry!	*(shake index finger—right hand)*
Says Pharaoh—	*(make crown on head)*
You Israelites	*(shake finger again)*
Are just too slow!	*(put emphasis and slowing down on last line)*

THE BURNING BUSH   Exodus 3:1–10

Near a high, high mountain,	*(touch finger tips)*
Moses saw a brightly burning bush.	*(cup hands)*
He quickly ran to see	
Why the fire did not go out!	*(spread hands in wonder)*
Then God spoke from the bush.	*(point index finger)*
You go down into Egypt	*(point down)*
Bring My people out	*(bring hands toward you)*
To the land I told you about!	

GOD AND PHARAOH   Exodus 5:1–2

God told Pharaoh	*(hold up index finger—left hand— for Pharaoh; point index finger—right hand—on a slant from heaven)*
"Let my people go."	*(emphasize each word with index finger—right hand)*
But Pharaoh said,	*(stiffen index finger—left hand)*
"Oh! no, no, no!"	*(shake head from side to side at each word)*

MEET MOSES' FAMILY   Exodus 6:20; 15:20

Little Moses says, Come and see   *(hold up all fingers—left hand;*
                                    point to little finger)

Who else is in my family:
Here's Amram, my father,   *(point to thumb)*
Jochebed, my mother,   *(point to index finger)*
Miriam, my sister,   *(point to middle finger)*
And Aaron, my brother.   *(point to ring finger)*
Now you count with me and see—   *(raise left hand higher)*
How many in our family!   *(count)*

HOW DID GOD LEAD THEM   Exodus 13:21–22

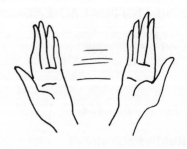

God led His people   *(point to heaven)*

During the day   *(spread hands—each to one side)*

36

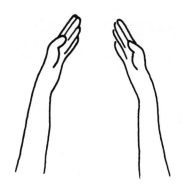

By a pillar of a cloud

(hold hands high with palms spread apart)

To show the way.
God led His people

(point to heaven)

During the night

(spread hands as before—only higher)

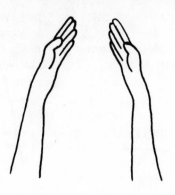

By a pillar of fire,   *(make a cloud pillar again)*

Shining this bright.   *(bend fingers back to indicate light rays)*

GOD TAKES CARE OF HIS PEOPLE   Exodus 14:15–20

The Israelites walked fast.   *(walk fingers of right hand quickly away from you)*

The enemy went faster!   *(raise fingers of left hand to indicate riders—move quickly after right hand)*

They asked Moses what to do.   *(spread hands in despair)*

So Moses prayed to God at once.   *(fold hands in prayer)*

God put a big thick cloud   *(hold hand upright—open and stiff)*

In front of Pharaoh all night;	*(put fingers—left hand behind "cloud")*
The cloud was so dark Pharaoh ,	*(make crown on head)*
Could not see one Israelite!	*(put left hand to eyes—try to see through "cloud")*

CROSSING THE RED SEA   Exodus 14:20-22

When the people came	*(walk where you stand)*
To the Red Sea,	
They did not know	*(stop walking)*
what to do;	
But a strong wind blew —	*(whoooo!)*
The waters went — whish!	*(sweep hand to right)*
And the people walked	*(resume walking)*
right through!	

NO WATER   Exodus 15:23–25

Israel could not drink	*(put hand to mouth as if drinking from a container)*
The waters of Marah.	*(take a sip)*
They were bitter as could be;	*(make wry face)*
God told Moses just how	*(point heavenward)*
To make the water sweet:	*(point as if instructing someone)*
Cut down a certain tree.	*(point to an imaginary tall "tree" then make arm upright—elbow bent let arm fall sideways as if into the waters)*

YUM! YUM!   YUM! YUM!   Exodus 16:14-15, 31

There's the manna, there's the manna,	*(point down)*
Down on the ground.	
Pick up some, pick up some,	*(put in jar)*
It's white and round.	
Eat some now, eat some now,	*(do so)*
Yum! Yum! Yum! Yum!	*(rub stomach)*

39

THE GOLDEN CALF   Exodus 32:1–4

The people said,
"Make us some gods!"   *(use demanding tone; point both
                                      thumbs at self)*
But Aaron made them only one;   *(hold up one index finger)*
A golden calf,   *(make fist of left hand for head;
                                      hold index finger and ring finger
                                      for ears)*
Made from earrings.   *(pretend to pull earrings off ears)*
They worshiped it   *(make "calf" again with left hand;
                                    *(bow right hand
When it was done.   toward left hand)*

WHAT ISRAEL DID   Exodus 32:7–8

Israel: *(stand up straight and stiffly)*
Stopped its ears,   *(put hands over ears)*
Closed its eyes,   *(close eyes)*
Turned its back   *(turn with back to child)*
On its God
In the skies.   *(put shoulders back in defiance)*

ISRAEL AND GOD   Exodus 32:8–10

Sometimes
They served God;   *(extend right arm up and left arm
                                      down for a seesaw)*
Sometimes   *(reverse arm position)*
They did not;
When they did,   *(return to original position)*
God blessed them;
But if not,   *(reverse above position)*
God did not!

THE TABLES OF STONE   Exodus 32:15–16

Up the mountain   *(walk two fingers of left hand up
                                      right arm; begin at wrist)*

Went Moses alone.   *(keep walking two fingers)*
There God gave him   *(point heavenward with pointer*
                                  finger of right hand)
Two tables of stone.   *(hold hands upright; side by side)*

A LONG WORD   Exodus 35:10

Tabernacle   *(hold up both hands—palms up)*
Is a long word   *(measure width with both hands)*
In the Old Testament;
But its meaning   *(raise measured word slightly)*
Is quite short   *(put hands much closer together)*
Just T-E-N-T, tent!   *(hold up four fingers of left hand,*
                                  point to each finger to
                                  spell the words)

TOO MANY GIFTS   Exodus 36:5–7

The people brought gifts   *(hold out hands as if giving)*
For the tabernacle.
(There were no stores to shop!)   *(spread hands wide)*
And they brought so much
Cloth, bracelets, and earrings,   *(measure yard; touch wrist, finger,*
                                  ears)
Moses had to say, STOP!   *(hold up hand in protest)*

THE ESCAPE   Joshua 2:15

Who helped the two spies?   *(hold up two fingers—right hand*
                                  for the spies)

Rahab, for she feared the Lord.   *(hold up index finger—left hand)*

How? Through a window,   *(form square with arms)*

She let them down by a cord.   *(lean forward—use hand over hand motion with cord)*

THE CORD   Joshua 2:18

How did the soldiers   *(spread hands and wiggle fingers for soldiers)*

Know Rahab's house   *(make a square with hands overlocked)*

In the city of Jericho?

By the scarlet cord   *(pretend to hold one end of hanging cord—hold hand high)*

Rahab had hung

In the middle of her window.   *(make a square with arms)*

THE MIRACLE AT THE JORDAN   Joshua 3:17

The priests waded in first,   *(move feet up down as if wading)*

At the side of the river,   *(hold hands flat—palms down, move from left to right as water moves)*

Holding the ark high;   *(put both hands up to right shoulder as if steadying the pole supporting the ark)*

Some waters piled up,   *(make a wall with the right hand up high)*

Some rolled away.   *(make rolling sweep of left hand)*

Look! the ground is dry!   *(point to ground)*

GOD SAVED HIS PEOPLE   Joshua 3:16–17

The priests stood still   *(plant feet more firmly)*

And the ground stayed dry,   *(point to ground—spread hands)*

While the people

Of God all marched by.   *(put hands at your sides—then spread fingers for people walking— "walk" fingers ahead of you)*

ONCE A DAY   Joshua 6:13–16

For six days   *(hold up six fingers)*

'Round the city wall   *(make wall of arms)*

The men marched

Once—that's all!   *(hold up pointer finger—left hand— then right hand for stop)*

The seventh day,	*(hold up seven fingers—wiggle seventh)*
'Round the city wall	*(make wall again)*
The men marched	
Seven times in all.	*(hold up seven fingers again)*

BLOW THE TRUMPET   Joshua 6:13

See the trumpet	*(hold up imaginary trumpet)*
The priests blew?	*(blow the imaginary trumpet)*
I can blow one.	*(pretend to blow it)*
How about you?	*(point to class)*

DEBORAH'S HOUSE   Judges 4:5

Friends who came	*(wide sweep with right arm)*
Deborah to see;	

Found her house	*(make fist of left hand)*

Under this palm tree.	*(hold right arm up; spread fingers to shade house)*

SAMSON HAD A SECRET   Judges 16:15–18

Samson had a secret;	*(put right hand over mouth)*
He kept it well,	*(keep hand over mouth)*
'Til he met Delilah.	*(hold up index finger—left hand)*
Her he did tell!	*(take hand away from mouth)*
She told wicked men	
For much, much money;	*(pretend to count money from one to the other)*
The men took Samson;	*(reach hands as if gripping someone)*
She took the money!	*(clutch money to self)*

SAMSON'S HAIR   Judges 16:17

Samson was strong	*(show muscle)*
While he had long hair;	
When it was short,	*(touch hair)*
His strength was just fair.	*(feel muscle; shake head)*

HOW DID SAMSON DIE?   Judges 16:29–30

Samson stood between two posts	*(hold arms straight up; stand stiffly)*
A hand on each one;	*(lower arms—pretend to place a hand against each pillar)*
He prayed,	*(bow head—close eyes; then bend shoulders forward)*
He pushed,	*(push hands against pillars)*
And down they came;	*(make pillars again and cross arms)*
Killing everyone.	*(hold bent arms over head as if protecting self from roof)*

TO A FIELD GOES RUTH   Ruth 2:2-3, 17

One, two, three, to a field went she;	*(three fingers)*
Four, five, six, the best field Ruth picks;	*(six fingers)*
Seven, eight, nine, its corn is fine;	*(nine fingers)*
Ten—how happy Ruth is then!	*(ten fingers)*

HANNAH'S WISH   I Samuel 1:9-11

This is Hannah praying   (praying hands)
To God up above.
See baby Samuel   (raise baby in arms)
God sent her to love?

THE NEW COAT   I Samuel 2:19

Hannah made Samuel   (sewing motions)
A new coat   (hold up coat)
Once—every—year.
Each time it was larger   (hold up larger coat)
As he grew,
Here—here—here!   (hands on hips; then
                                    shoulders; then two
                                    inches above head)

WHAT DID SAMUEL DO?   I Samuel 3:3-5

Samuel opened   (hold hands up, palms
                                    together)

The temple doors wide,   (open hands outward)
To let God's people
Go inside.   (walk fingers along arm)

HOW SOON?   I Samuel 3:5–10

One night Samuel   (asleep on hand)
Heard God call.
He jumped to answer.   (awake with a start)
Just like ————   (snap fingers or clap hands)

TALL KING SAUL   I Samuel 9:1–2

This king is named Saul.   (hold up index finger of
                                    left hand)

How tall did he grow?   (lift finger slightly)
None reached his shoulders   (point about shoulder high on
                                    finger)

Even on tiptoe!   (rise on tiptoes)

I AM SAUL   I Samuel 17:23; 18:10

I am Saul.   *(point to self)*
I am the king.   *(set crown on your head)*

            (take one step to the right)

I am David.   *(point to self)*
I like to sing.   *(nod)*

            (step back to first position)

Sometimes I'm sad,   *(unsmiling)*
Sometimes I'm gay.   *(smile)*

            (step to right again)

When he is sad,   *(point to Saul)*
I sing and play.   *(strum harp)*

DAVID'S HARP   I Samuel 16:16-18, 23

Let's make David's harp.   *(crook left arm upwards)*
See the strings?   *(strum strings)*
He plays the harp   *(do so)*
While he sings.

SLEEPY SHEEP   I Samuel 16:11

Sh! Sh! Be still!   *(finger to lips)*
Here's David's sheep.   *(hold up fingers)*
They feel so safe
They've gone to sleep.   *(softly)*

GOLIATH   I Samuel 17:23-24

There was a big man   *(hold up index finger)*

Who stood tall, t-a-l-l,

(measure hands as high as you can reach)

Saul's men were afraid

(hug self as if trembling—look up to giant)

He was so tall, t-a-l-l!

(repeat first action)

BRAVE DAVID   I Samuel 17:34-35

A lamb one day	*(make left fist;*
	jump it around)
Did play, play, play.	
A lion to the sheep	*(make right fist;*
	inch it toward lamb)
Did creep, creep, creep.	
From behind a clump,	*(pounce lion on lamb)*
He did jump, jump, jump.	
Grabbing the sheep,	*(lion grips lamb)*
He did leap, leap, leap.	*(make fist give one leap)*
But David the shepherd,	*(use index finger*
	of left hand)
Did hurry, hurry, hurry.	*(move to lion)*
The lion he did grab	
And stab, stab, stab.	*(stab lion with index finger)*

TWO FRIENDS   I Samuel 18:1-3

This is Jonathan,	*(hold up left index finger)*
This is David;	*(hold up right index finger)*
Friends from the start.	*(hook fingers)*
How do I know this?	
They never liked	
To be apart!	*(pretend you cannot*
	unhook them)

THE BEAUTIFUL TEMPLE   I Kings 6:1, 21

See the beautiful temple?	*(arms bent for rectangle)*
It shines in the sun.	
It was built for God	*(raise arms in praise)*
By King Solomon.	*(set crown on your head)*

49

THE WHIRLWIND II Kings 1:11–12

Elijah,	*(hold up index finger—right hand)*
Elisha,	*(hold up index finger—left hand)*
Were walking	*(walk two sets of fingers—side by side)*
And talking;	
When a chariot of fire	*(make a fist of one hand; hold high)*
Came flying down from heaven.	*(swoop the chariot down; then hold up two index fingers side by side and jerk the fingers apart)*
A whirlwind split them.	*(make downward sweep of left hand)*
Took Elijah up to heaven.	*(move Elijah up high to the right)*

ELIJAH AND THE RAVENS I Kings 17:6

The ravens flew down	*(flap arms)*
With bread and meat,	*(hold out left hand; then right)*
Two times a day —	*(hold up two fingers)*
So Elijah could eat.	*(eat)*

THE BROOK I Kings 17:7

See the brook	*(hands wide apart)*
Where Elijah drank?	*(drink from hands)*
No rain fell,	
And it shrank and shrank!	*(arms wide again; put closer twice)*

THE POOR WIDOW I Kings 17:10-16

A little meal,	*(extend left hand)*
A little oil,	*(pour with right hand)*
Were all the widow had.	
Elijah spoke then,	
And suddenly —	*(blink eyes once)*
The widow was so glad!	
Just see the meal!	*(make two scoops with left hand)*

Just see the oil!   (pour longer)
A miracle no doubt.
Whatever she ate,   (eat)
(And her son, too)
The food did not give out!   (repeat scoops of meal
                                       and pouring)

THE LITTLE BOY   I Kings 17:17-23

Meet the widow,   (raise right index finger)
And her little boy.   (show thumb — right hand)
How happy they were!
One day he died,   (close thumb)
But Elijah prayed —   (bow head)
Back he was with her!   (thumb pop out)

THE NICE SURPRISE   II Kings 4:8-11

Come and see the room   (beckon with finger)
They built for Elisha.
My, what a nice surprise!   (clasp hands)
    A table, a stool,   (count furniture)
        A candlestick, a bed.
Wide will he open his eyes!   (do so)

NAAMAN   II Kings 5:10-14

One, two, three,   (count on left hand)
Not well yet!   (shake head)

51

Four, five, six,   (count)

Still just wet!   (hold dripping hands)

One time more —   (one finger; then six)
Seven; look!   (seven fingers)
Not one sore!   (point to feet, arms, face)

THE BOY KING   II Chronicles 34:1–3

Only eight   (hold up eight fingers)
Was Josiah
When he was made king.   (cup hands for crown on head)
He turned not
To the left   (hold out left hand stiffly
                                       to the left)

Nor to the right   (hold out right hand stiffly
                                       to the right)

But followed God   (touch palms and point them
                                       straight ahead)

In everything.
While a boy!

WHAT DID HE FIND?   II Chronicles 34:14–16

The priest in the temple	*(make rectangular building)*
Was cleaning all around;	*(pretend to sweep with broom)*
When all of a sudden,	*(clap hands lightly)*
What do you think he found?	
The holy book of God.	*(fold hands like a book)*
What a happy thing!	
The scribe ran quickly	*(run two fingers along arm)*
And took it to the king!	*(cup hands for crown)*
The king was glad too!	*(clap hands again lightly)*
And sent right away	*(point finger in command)*
For the people to come hear	
God's Book that same day.	*(cup both hands to ears)*

WILLING HANDS   Nehemiah 4:17

This hand builds the wall	*(hold out right hand)*
With all its might;	*(make fist)*
This hand holds a sword;	*(hold out left hand)*
Ready to fight!	*(put hand as if on sword at side)*

THE SIGNAL   Nehemiah 4:20

Far apart were the men	*(hold hands about two feet apart; with index fingers up)*
As they built the city wall;	
They stopped work to help fight,	*(hold sword)*
When they heard the trumpet call!	*(pretend to blow trumpet)*

THE WALL IS DONE   Nehemiah 6:15–16

The wall was done	*(hold hands for wall)*
In fifty-two days.	*(raise hands five times, then raise two fingers)*
Who helped them do it?	*(spread hands in inquiry)*
To God went the praise!	*(raise hands in thanks)*

THE NEW QUEEN   Esther 2:16-17

Esther, Esther,   *(address index finger)*
Please tell me, do —
Why do you look so gay?

Because, because,   *(raise finger slightly)*
The king chose *me*   *(raise finger slightly)*
To be his queen today!   *(make crown on your head)*

SEE ESTHER'S CROWN?   Esther 2:17

See *Esther's crown —   *(hold out crown)*
    all shiny and new?
I can wear it—well,   *(put crown on your head)*
    how about you?

*Substitute kings' names

SAD JOB   Job 2:11

Boils, boils,   *(hold out hands and look at them)*
From head to feet   *(touch head and point to feet)*
Sad Job had one day.
His three friends came   *(hold up three fingers)*
To comfort him,   *(hold right hand as if on Job's
                                             shoulder)*

Each in his own way.

HAPPY JOB   Job 41:12

God blessed Job,   *(spread hands in a blessing)*
Took away his boils   *(examine hands as if healed)*
And made him rich again   *(spread hands—palms up)*
He gave Job
Seven sons, three daughters,   *(hold up seven fingers—add three
                                             more)*

Oh, what a happy man!   *(clasp hands in joy)*

WHICH KING?   Psalm 43:4; I Samuel 16:23

Which king a harp did play,   *(bend right arm stiffly for harp;*
                                    play harp with left hand)

And sang God's praise all day?   *(hold mouth briefly as if singing)*
   —DAVID.   *(repeat after hesitation)*

WHAT DID ISAIAH DO?   Isaiah 11:1—5

Isaiah was a good man.   *(Hold up index finger—left hand)*
What did Isaiah do?
He wrote much about one man   *(pretend to write)*
I'll spell His name for you.   *(beckon with right index finger)*
   J-e-s-u-s.

JEREMIAH   Jeremiah 14:3

Some bad men   *(hold up right hand—palm toward*
                                    you)

Put Jeremiah   *(hold up thumb of left hand)*
Into a pit;   *(clap right hand over left as*
                                    thumb goes inside)

Some good men   *(hold up right hand—palm away*
                                    from you)

Came along later   *(close right hand down over left*
                                    hand)

Pulled him out of it!   *(remove right hand—let thumb pop*
                                    up)

SEE DANIEL PRAY?   Daniel 6:10

See Daniel's house?   *(make roof)*
See Daniel pray?   *(praying hands)*
When does he pray?
Three times a day!   *(raise three fingers)*

GOD TOOK CARE OF DANIEL   Daniel 6:21-22

See the lions?   *(two fists)*
Ready to bite?   *(open fists slightly;*
                                       snap at air)

But God himself   *(look up)*
Shut their mouths tight!   *(shut fists tightly)*

THE TEN-DAY TEST   Daniel 1:11-16

For ten days,   *(hold up all fingers)*
Daniel and his friends   *(close six fingers)*
Did water drink   *(pretend to drink with one hand*
And then pulse eat.   *and eat with the other)*
Their faces
Were fatter so they   *(indicate fat cheeks)*
Did not have to eat   *(fold arms across chest)*
The king's meat.

JONAH RAN AWAY   Jonah 1:1-3

God sent Jonah to Nineveh   *(admonish with index finger)*
Told him just what to say;
But Jonah did not   *(shake head vigorously)*
     want to go —
He ran the other way!   *(turn around)*

JONAH AND THE FISH   Jonah 1:17; 2:10

Down went Jonah,   *(Dive index finger —*
                                       left hand)
Up came the fish;   *(Bring right hand up)*
In went Jonah   *(right hand "swallow"*
                                       Jonah)

With a big swish!

On swam the fish   *(swim hand back and forth)*
Till God's command:
spit Jonah out   *(pop finger up and over)*
On the dry land.

56

JONAH WAS LUCKY   Jonah 2:1-3

Jonah was lucky,   *(hold up index finger —*
                                    right hand)

(And this I do mean!)   *(nod head)*
He rode in a fish —   *(palms together; thumbs*
                                    out for fins)

The first submarine!   *(dive downward; then*
                                    level off)

SECTION THREE
NEW TESTAMENT FINGER PLAYS

COUNT THE FOUR BOOKS

One book, two books,

(hold up two fingers) in turn)

Three books, four,

(four fingers)

Tell of one Jesus,

(hold up index finger of other hand)

And no more!

(shake head)

HIS STAR   Matthew 2:1-2, 9-11

The wise men came
    from afar.
Guess what led them?
    Jesus' star!

*(hold right hand out flat; move
    slowly from right to left)*
*(left hand high above
    right; wiggle fingers)*

COUNT THEM   Matthew 2:11

Gifts from the wise men —
Come and see.
Count the gifts with me:
One—two—three!

(hold out hands; palms up)
(beckon with fingers)

(count on fingers)

FOLLOW ME   Matthew 4:18-20

Jesus said,
"Follow me."
*Peter did,
As quick as —

(beckon with finger)
(take one step)
(clap hands once)

*Other apostles' names can be used

JESUS COULD DO ANYTHING   Matthew 8:26-27

The wind blew and blew,
But Jesus spoke,

And the wind stopped —
    just like that!
The waves rolled and rolled,
But Jesus spoke,
And the high waves —
    just went flat!

*(hold up index finger
    of right hand)*
(clap hands once)

(rolling motions of a wave)
(index finger again)
(stop rolling motion)

THE NUMBER-ONE GUEST   Matthew 9:9; Luke 5:29

Matthew had many friends,

Jesus was his very best,
Matthew gave a great feast

With Jesus the number-one guest.

*(hold up all fingers; weave back
    and forth)*
(hold up index finger—right hand)
*(spread hands, palms down, sideway
    as if smoothing a table cloth)*
(elevate right index finger again)

HOW MANY BLIND MEN?   Matthew 9:27-30

How many blind men   *(make square with arms)*
   went into the house?
This many!   *(two fingers)*
   Jesus touched   *(lay hand over man's*
     this man's eyes;   *eyes at left)*
   Then he touched   *(repeat at right side)*
     this man's eyes.
How many blind men
   came out of the house?
Not any!   *(shut the two fingers or*
                      make zero sign)

JESUS DID GOOD   Matthew 12:9-13

His left hand is well,   *(hold out left hand)*
His right hand is sick;   *(hold right hand stiffly*
                        at side)

Then Jesus spoke once —
Now which one is sick?   *(hold out both hands)*

THE HAPPY FAMILY   Matthew 13:54-56

This is Joseph, the carpenter,   *(hold up one finger,*
                        left hand)

This is Mary, his wife,   *(two fingers)*
And this is Jesus —   *(three fingers)*
   that makes three;
This? His brothers — four;   *(four fingers)*
This? His sisters —   *(thumb)*
   two or more.
There! What a happy   *(close right hand around*
   family!   *left hand)*

63

HOW MANY HAVE YOU? Matthew 13:55–56

Four brothers Jesus had.   *(hold up four fingers right hand)*

And sisters? At least two.   *(hold up two fingers, left hand)*

Now how many brothers   *(lower hands)*

And sisters, too, have you?   *(point to class)*

JESUS LOVED THE CHILDREN   Matthew 19:13–15

Mothers and daddies   *(hold up all fingers of left hand—*
                                   then right hand)
Brought their children   *(measure several heights of*
                                   children's heads with palm
                                   of right hand)
For Jesus to bless,   *(hold out both hands, palms down, as*
                                   if on head of a child)
How many children   *(spread hands—palms up)*
Were brought to Him?
We can only guess!   *(point to self)*

WHAT WAS THE TEMPLE?   Matthew 21:12–13; Mark 11:15–16

The temple   *(make square with arms)*
Was the house of God;
Worship went on inside.   *(raise hands heavenward)*
Twice Jesus   *(hold up two fingers)*
Saw some bad men there
And drove them all outside.   *(hold imaginary whip in hand, make*
                                   sweeping motion)

ONLY FIVE   Matthew 25:1–13

One, two, three, four, five   *(let each finger pop up on left*
                                   hand)
Foolish virgins late did arrive;
Six, seven, eight, nine, ten.   *(let rest of fingers pop up)*
But they had to go
Back home again!   *(shake head sadly)*

DID JESUS SING TO GOD?   Matthew 26:20, 30

Did Jesus sing to God?   *(make book)*
Did his disciples too?

Oh, yes, they all   *(nod head)*
    sang hymns —
As *you* and *I* can do.   *(point to self; then, others)*

MENDING THEIR NETS   Mark 1:19

See the fish net.   *(pretend to hold one up with both*
    hands)
And see all the holes,   *(point with left hand to two places*
    in the net)

That the big fish tore?
So James and John   *(hold up two fingers of right hand)*
Mended back and forth.   *(pretend to use a shuttle back and*
    forth on hanging net)

There are holes no more!   *(hold net up for close inspection;*
    shake head)

HOW DID THEY GET IN?   Mark 2:3-4

These are the friends,   *(hold up four fingers —*
    right hand)
This is the sick man   *(hold out flat — index*
    finger, left hand)

They took to Jesus one day.
The house was so full
They went to the roof,   *(raise index finger slowly*
    — still flat)
And let the bed in that way.   *(lower sick man slowly)*

TWO BY TWO   Mark 6:7

Jesus sent the disciples   *(shake one finger in command)*
Two by two;   *(walk two fingers of each hand)*
To tell the people   *(stop one pair; then the other;*
What to do.   *then move on)*

LOOKING FOR THE MASTER   Mark 6:33–34

Up a hill, down a hill—   *(walk two fingers up and down hill*
                                                                made by arm and elbow)
Looking for the Master.   *(hold hand over eyes as if looking)*
There He is! There He is!   *(point)*
Then the man runs faster.   *(run fingers faster)*

HERE'S SOME FISH   * Mark 6:41

Here's some fish, and   *(hand to people sitting*
   here's some fish,   *on the ground)*
Now have some bread.   *(repeat action)*
Eat some fish,   *(eating motions)*
   and eat some bread,
After thanks are said.   *(bow head)*

                                    *Use also with Mark 8:6

BARTIMAEUS   Mark 10:46–52

Bartimaeus, Bartimaeus,   *(put hands over eyes—turn slightly*
                                                              to the right)
Whom *FIRST* did you see?   *(uncover quickly—blink as if at*
                                                              some one in front of you)
Jesus Himself,   *(turn slightly to the left as if*
                                                              blind man answers)
Looking at me.   *(point to self)*

TWO MITES   Mark 12:41-44

Count: one mite, two mites,   *(circle fingers for coins)*
Were all the widow had.
She gave both to God,   *(drop in collection)*
And then she was so glad.   *(clasp hands in joy)*

NAMING THE BABY   Luke 1:26, 31

Our mothers named *us,*   *(point to self)*
Our fathers named *us,*
But God himself named   *(point to heaven)*
The baby Jesus.   *(cradle baby)*

NO ROOM AT THE INN Luke 2:7

No room at the inn?   *(spread hands in dismay)*
Where did baby Jesus stay?   *(cradle baby)*
Why in a manger   *(lay baby down)*
Filled with the softest of hay. *(pat hay)*

WHAT DID THE SHEPHERDS SEE?   Luke 2:8-16

See, see?   *(point to sky)*
What did the shepherds see?
   Angels shining in a light!
Hear, hear!   *(cup ear)*
What did the shepherds hear?
   Angels singing in the night.
Walk, walk!   *(walk where you stand)*
Where did the shepherds go?
   To the town of Bethlehem.
Look, look!   *(point to manger)*
What did the shepherds find?
   Baby Jesus — that same
     night!

THE SHEPHERD Luke 2:15-17

Here goes a shepherd   *(walk fingers quickly along
      arm)*

To find the manger;
Here he comes back again,   *(walk fingers back quickly)*
Telling each stranger!

THE HAPPY SMILE Luke 2:25-30

Look at Simeon's face!   *(point)*
Why the happy smile?
He's holding baby Jesus   *(cradle baby)*
In his arms a while.   *(smile at baby)*

THE TEMPLE   Luke 2:25-28

This is the temple,   *(all fingertips touching)*
And every day
The people come   *(walk fingers before you)*
To sing and pray.   *(praying hands)*

THE MISSING BOY   Luke 2:43–44

There goes Joseph,   *(hold up index finger—right hand; move it slowly straight away from you)*

There goes Mary,   *(move other index finger along beside "Joseph")*

Walking along   *(continue moving fingers)*
At the day's end,
Both of them know   *(stop fingers)*
Something is wrong;
They look up here,   *(turn both fingers to the right)*
They look back there,   *(turn both fingers to the left)*
No Jesus anywhere!   *(spread hands wide)*

WHERE WAS THE BOY JESUS?   Luke 2:46-47

Joseph and Mary were   *(hold up index fingers)*
    worried;
Back to the city they hurried.   *(move fingers to right quickly)*

Looked on the street —

(hand at forehead; look at passersby)

Looked in each store —

(do so)

Looked in the temple —

(look straight ahead)

Stop! Look no more!

(stop signal with hand)

Where did they find the boy Jesus?

(spread hands in question)

In God's house—where God looks for *us*.

(point to self; then, class)

70

THE BOY JESUS GREW   Luke 2:52

Taller and taller   *(measure hand higher and higher)*
The boy Jesus grew;   *(continue raising hand)*
Each day He pleased God   *(point upward with right index
                                        finger)*
And the people   *(point upward with left index
    too.   finger)*

PETER HAD A BOAT   Luke 5:3

Peter had a boat —   *(hold hands together —
                                        slightly opened)*

It was very strong.
The wind blew the sail,   *(hold up index finger)*
Moving the boat along.   *(move boat along)*

When there was no wind,
His boat would not go.   *(stop boat)*
What did Peter do?
He would row, row, row.   *(rowing motions)*

THE BROKEN NET   Luke 5:4-6

Peter fished all night long   *(hold up index finger)*
But — no fish in the net!   *(interlock fingers for net)*
Jesus said, "Cast again."
The fish *broke* Peter's net!   *(pull hands apart)*

DID JESUS PRAY?   Luke 6:12

Jesus prayed each day   *(fold hands in prayer)*
Whether cloudy or bright;   *(spread hands)*
Anywhere, anytime.   *(hold out left hand—palm up; then
                                        right palm)*
Sometimes He prayed all night!   *(fold hands again)*

71

SIMON THE PHARISEE   Luke 7:36–45

Jesus went	*(walk two fingers of right hand)*
To Simon's house	*(touch all finger tips for roof)*
Who had invited Him to eat.	*(eating motions)*
Simon gave	*(hold up index finger—left hand)*
No kiss at all,	*(kiss hand)*
Nor water for His feet.	*(hold bowl of water)*
But someone—	
Who? The sinner	
Did wash His feet.	*(point to feet)*

TWELVE YEARS OLD   Luke 8:54-55

Jairus had one child.	*(hold up right index finger)*
She was very sick.	*(let finger fall)*
Till Jesus came and took	
her hand.	
Said Jesus, "Maid, arise."	
Open flew her eyes —	*(shut your eyes; then open)*
Now see how well the	*(raise right index finger)*
girl could stand!	

THE GOOD SAMARITAN   Luke 10:38-40

Some robbers beat a man	*(hold up right index finger)*
And left him to die.	*(finger fall)*
A priest and a Levite	
Saw him but walked on by.	*(walk fingers quickly along arm)*
A good Samaritan	*(hold up left index finger)*
Came along that way;	
Looked and then stopped	*(stop finger)*
quickly;	
Helped him right away.	*(pour oil over one hand)*

JESUS' THREE FRIENDS   Luke 10:30-37

In this house,   *(touch finger tips for roof)*
There lived three;   *(three fingers)*
Mary, Martha and Lazarus.
Who knew them?
Who loved them?   *(hand on heart)*
That is right! Who else
    but Jesus?

THE BENT WOMAN   Luke 13:10-13

There was a woman   *(raise index finger)*
Who was bent like this.   *(bend finger)*
She could not straighten at all.   *(fail to straighten finger)*
But Jesus touched her
And then what happened?
She could stand up straight   *(straighten finger)*
    and tall!

THE MONEY BAG   Luke 15:14-16

This is the younger brother,   *(index finger of right hand)*

Spending his money.   *(count coins from one
                                            hand to other)*

73

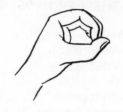

Is his money bag empty?   *(hold up bag by top corners)*

Shake it well and see!   *(do so; nod head)*

THE TEN LEPERS   Luke 17:11-19

Here are ten lepers —   *(show ten fingers)*
Jesus healed *all* the men.   *(raise hands slightly)*
How many thanked him?
Just *one* out of the ten.   *(hold up one finger)*

WHICH DID GOD HEAR?   Luke 18:10–14

Two men   *(hold both index fingers)*
Stood to pray;
One loved himself,   *(point to self with one finger)*
And one loved God.   *(point to heaven with other finger)*
Two men   *(hold both fingers side by side)*
Stood to pray,
Which of the two
Was heard that day?   *(pause in questioning attitude;*
                              then raise finger for good man)

74

ZACCHAEUS   Luke 19:1-6

Up, up, the tree,	*(climb with both hands)*
Went short, short Zacchaeus;	
'Round, 'round he looked	*(hand to forehead)*
Till he saw him — Jesus!	*(point downward gladly)*

HURRY, ZACCHAEUS!   Luke 19:4-6

Hurry, Zacchaeus!	*(beckon to him up in the tree)*
Climb down the tree!	*(pretend to climb down by hands)*
Today in your house	*(make square with hands)*
Will Jesus be.	

SIX WATERPOTS   John 1:11

Here are six waterpots	*(hold up six fingers)*
All along in a line.	
Jesus did a miracle—	*(bend fingers as if pouring)*
The water became wine!	*(spread hands in surprise)*

TWO BROTHERS   John 1:40-42

Andrew, why do you walk	*(walk two fingers of right hand straight away from you slowly)*
Faster and faster?	*(walk fingers faster)*
To take my brother Peter,	*(put two fingers of left hand beside Andrew then walk two steps toward left side)*
To meet the Master.	

THE WATERPOT   John 4:6-8, 28

See the waterpot	*(bend arm; hold hand upright)*
The woman had?	
She went to the well one day.	
Who asked for a drink?	*(raise waterpot)*
Jesus himself!	
Did the woman turn away?	

THE SICK BOY   John 4:46-53

Jesus was in *this* town;   *(hold index finger to far right)*
The sick boy, in *this* one.   *(other index finger far left)*
    Who could heal him?
    What could be done?
Jesus spoke in *this* town;   *(raise that finger slightly)*
The sick boy? healed   *(raise other finger)*
    that day!
    Jesus healed him,
    Though far away.   *(hands farther apart)*

THE LAME MAN   John 5:5-9

This is the bed   *(hold left hand flat—palm up*
                         for a mat)

Of the lame man,   *(lay index finger of left hand*
                         on bed)

Who heard the people talk;
Then Jesus came   *(turn head and move eyes as if he*
                         walked)

And said to him,
"Take up thy bed, and walk."
And—he—did!   *(at the word* and *stand the man up)*
                         (at the word he *close fingers of left*
                         hand and place beside "man")
                         (at the word did *move man and*
                         bed-roll along quickly)

FIVE LOAVES — TWO FISHES   John 6:5-12

Five loaves of bread,   *(hold up five fingers)*
And two small fish,   *(hold up two fingers —*
                         other hand)

Were given by a lad.   *(extend hands with gifts)*
Jesus gave thanks,   *(praying hands)*
Five thousand ate —   *(eat)*
See what food they still had!   *(hold up loaded arms)*

76

THE BLIND MAN   John 9:1-7

Jesus mixed, mixed the clay;   *(mix clay)*
Patted it on the man's eyes.   *(do so)*
The man washed his eyes—   *(wash your eyes)*
Now he could see the skies!   *(look up gladly — hands
                                       raised in praise)*

LAZARUS   John 11:44–47

One, two, three, four, five   *(count off fingers on left hand)*

Jesus made Lazarus alive;
Six, seven, eight, nine, ten   *(hold up right hand—pop up
                                       fingers as you count)*

He was with his sisters again.   *(give a soft clap of joy)*

BRANCHES FOR JESUS   John 12:12-13

Here are the palm trees,   *(arms high)*
Standing very tall;
Chop! Chop! go the axes,   *(chop branch)*
Down, down the branches   *(eyes follow one fall).*
    fall!

Why put the branches   *(spread on ground)*
Along the road — thus?
To make the road pretty
For the Lord Jesus!   *(clasp hand)*

COUNT THE DAYS   John 19:17–18; Matthew 12:40

Jesus died on the cross   *(make a letter T)*
For you and for me.   *(point to class; then, self)*
How long was he buried?   *(spread hands)*
Count the days; 1, 2, 3.   *(count sadly)*

WHY DO YOU CRY?   John 20:13–18

Why do you cry   *(wipe tears from eyes)*
Mary Magdalene?   *(address index finger)*
Jesus died with much pain.   *(raise finger slightly)*

Why do you smile   *(make smile with fingers)*
Mary Magdalene?   *(raise finger again)*
Jesus, my friend, lives again!   *(clap hands softly)*

BREAKFAST WITH JESUS   John 21:1-2, 9-13

Build a fire.   *(put coals on fire)*
Then cook some fish;   *(lay each on fire)*
    some bread.
Add some coals to keep   *(add a few)*
    the heat.

See the breakfast   *(point to food)*
That Jesus had ready
To give his disciples to eat?

✓THE ASCENSION   Acts 1:2, 9–12

1, 2, 3, 4, 5   *(count fingers)*
Jesus went to heaven alive
6, 7, 8, 9, 10,   *(finish finger counting)*
He's coming back to earth again.   *(clap hands softly)*

THEN THERE WERE TWELVE   Acts 1:23–26

There were twelve apostles   *(hold up ten fingers—then two)*
Until Judas died;   *(hold up left index finger)*
Then there were eleven.   *(hold up ten fingers—then one)*
So, they chose Matthias   *(cast lot)*
To take Judas' place   *(hold up left index finger)*
Then there were twelve again.   *(hold up ten fingers—then two)*

WHO DID IT FIRST?   Acts 2:14, 37–41

Who preached the gospel   *(spread hands)*
The very first time   *(hold up one finger)*
And where? In Jerusalem.
One of the twelve apostles—

*Finger
PLAYS*

ON PENTECOST   Acts 2:41

I have ten fingers.	*(hold up ten fingers)*
Is that enough	
To show the number baptized?	*(shake head)*
I show three fingers,	*(hold up three fingers)*
Then three zeros—	*(repeat three circles in a row—one thumb and finger)*
3,000 were baptized.	*(repeat number-action)*

A LAME MAN   Acts 3;1-8

A lame man	
Sat begging for money —	*(hold out hand)*
Holding out his hand.	
Peter said,	*(hold up index finger— right hand)*
In the name of Jesus,	
Now you can stand!	*(pull man to feet)*

WHAT DID BARNABAS DO?   Acts 4:36–37

There goes Barnabas	*(walk fingers away)*
To sell his land	*(spread wide flat hands)*
To help the poor to eat.	
Here comes Barnabas	*(walk fingers back)*
With the money	*(cup coins in hands)*
To put at the apostles' feet.	*(empty cup on ground)*

THE FIRST TO DIE   Acts 7:57–60

See the big stones	*(hold up closed fists)*
The men did throw	*(throw stones)*
To hit Stephen's head?	*(tap head)*
What did he do?	
He prayed and prayed	*(fold hands)*
Until he was dead.	*(drop hands—bow head)*

HERE COMES THE CHARIOT   Acts 8:30–37

Here comes the chariot   *(hold open hands together, thumbs*
  up the road.   * hidden, move slowly along)*
See Philip and the eunuch inside?   *(raise right thumb—then left thumb)*
Philip preaches the word.   *(wiggle right thumb)*
Then the chariot stops.   *(stop hands moving)*
The eunuch's baptized.   *(close thumbs)*
As fast as it can;
There goes the chariot down   *(move chariot on by)*
  the road.
Home goes the eunuch—
A happy man!   *(raise left thumb—wiggle)*

HOW LONG WAS SAUL BLIND?   Acts 9:8–9, 17–18

One day,   *(point to fingers as you count)*
Two days,
Three days went by—
Saul was blind as could be;   *(cover eyes)*
Then came
To Saul—
Ananias;
The scales fell, and Saul   *(flutter fingers downward;*
  could see.   * then open closed eyes)*

HELLO, APOSTLE PAUL   Acts 9:15, 18

Hello, apostle Paul.   *(extend right hand)*
Glad to meet you.   *(shake hands)*
You love God and Jesus —   *(point to other)*
And *I* do too.   *(point to self)*

HOW DID PAUL ESCAPE?   Acts 9:23–25

The walls of Damascus   *(hold arms high)*
Were high, high,   *(raise still higher)*
And very wide;   *(spread hands flat)*

Paul's friends let his basket   *(circle arms horizontally)*
Down, down, down,   *(lower rope)*
Over the side.

DORCAS   Acts 9:36-42

This is Dorcas;   *(hold up index finger)*
One day she died —   *(lay finger on open hand)*
All her friends were sad.
Then Peter prayed;   *(bow head)*
God made her live —   *(raise up Dorcas finger)*
All her friends were glad!   *(clasp hands gladly)*

PAUL AND SILAS   Acts 16:19-26

Once Paul and Silas   *(hold up thumbs)*
Two men of God —
Were put in jail one day.   *(put thumbs down into*
                                          closed fists)
A mighty earthquake   *(bob fists up and down)*
Broke their chains,   *(thumbs pop up)*
For God had heard   *(praying hands)*
      them pray.

PETER AND THE ANGEL   Acts 12:6–9

One, two, what did the angel do?   *(count off on fingers*
Three, four, woke Peter on the floor; *as you go)*
Five, six, then his sandals did fix.
Seven, eight, open swung the gate,
Nine, ten, Peter was free again!

WHY DID PETER STAY OUT?   Acts 12:12–16

Now here is the gate   *(draw a big square)*
Outside Mary's house.
Peter knocked and knocked.   *(knock three times)*

Why did he stay out?
Rhoda ran inside—   *(run two fingers)*
In her hurry—left gate locked!   *(push gate)*

THE THREE FRIENDS   Acts 18:1–3

This is Aquila,   *(point to first finger, left hand)*
This is Priscilla,   *(point to second finger)*
And this, the apostle Paul;   *(point to third finger)*
All were tentmakers,   *(hold three fingers higher, then*
                                        make tent)
All the best of friends,   *(close fingers of right hand*
                                        around three fingers)
But they loved God the most of all. *(point index finger—right hand—up)*

THE TENT   Acts 18:1-6

This is the tent   *(touch index fingers and*
                                        thumbs)
That Paul made   *(sew)*
From cloth and pieces   *(hold up cloth)*
   of cord;
This is the money   *(hold out money)*
People paid —
Paul gave it all to the Lord.   *(drop in collection plate)*

THE YOUNG MAN   Acts 20:9–10

While Paul was preaching   *(point finger at class)*
Eutychus went to sleep   *(close eyes; hands by cheek)*
In this high window.   *(make square with arms)*
He fell and died.
But Paul raised him right up.
Did he fall asleep again? *NO!*

PAUL'S SHIP   Acts 27:1–2, 17

Here is Paul's ship.   *(hold right hand—cup slightly)*

To make it go,
Run the sail up;   *(touch right hand—fingertips to
                                        center of boat)*

*GOODBYE, PAUL   Acts 27:1-2

There goes Paul   *(point)*
In a big ship.
Goodbye, Paul!   *(wave)*
Have a good trip!

*May substitute Timothy or Titus

Why does Paul
Sail far away?
To go preach
God's holy Way.

(point to distance)

(admonishing finger)

Let the wind blow!

(blow on sail)

PAUL AND THE SNAKE   Acts 28:1–3

Down Paul laid sticks on the fire;   *(lay sticks—with hands)*
Up came a snake   *(wiggle right arm)*
And grabbed Paul by the hand.   *(bite left hand and hold)*
Did it hurt? and did Paul die? NO!
He shook it off—   *(shake left hand)*
In the fire it did land!   *(point to fire)*

TIMOTHY, TIMOTHY   II Timothy 1:5

Timothy, Timothy,   *(address index finger)*
Why so happy?
My mother is reading to me!

Timothy, Timothy,   *(raise finger high)*
What have you heard?   *(lower finger again)*
A story from God's holy   *(raise finger again)*
    Word!

HEAVEN   Revelation 21:4

In heaven   *(point up)*
I now do know;   *(point to self)*
There will be—
No tears,   *(count each time—shake head)*
No death,
No pain.
To heaven   *(point up)*
I want to go!   *(point to self—nod head)*

HOW MANY LIARS?   Revelation 21:8

How many liars   *(spread fingers)*
To heaven will go?   *(point up)*
The Bible tells us   *(hold open book)*
So we will know—   *(lay book down)*
Not one!   *(hold zero high)*

THE OPEN GATES   Revelation 21:22–25

God opened the   *(point up)*
Gates of His heaven *wide*—   *(spread hands—open them)*
To let all
His people come inside.   *(walk all fingers along)*

WILL THE SUN SHINE?   Revelation 21:23

Will the sun shine   *(hold up circle)*
In heaven some day?
Please! I want to know!   *(point to self)*
No, the sun won't shine!   *(shake head)*
The glory of God   *(point up)*
Will make heaven glow!   *(make sweep with open hands)*

WHOSE NAME IS LAST?   Revelation 22:21

Whose name is last   *(hold up closed book)*
In all the Bible?
The one Holy Book.   *(hold up one finger)*
The name? Jesus!   *(point up)*
In the *last* verse.   *(turn book over—point to it)*
Now *you* come and look!   *(open book and extend to class)*

SECTION FOUR
GENERAL FINGER PLAYS

DRAW A BIG SQUARE

First, draw a big, BIG square   *(draw with fingers)*
Then cut it in two.   *(draw vertical line down the middle)*
Here is the Old Testament   *(point to left half)*
And here is the New.   *(point to right half)*

HOW MANY JUDGES?

Fifteen judges   *(hold up ten fingers; then five)*
Called by Jehovah;   *(look heavenward)*
All men but one;   *(hold up one finger)*
Her name? Deborah.   *(hold palms close together at
                                    beginning; move apart some at
                                    each syllable of her name)*

THE THREE KINGS

There were three kings   *(hold up three fingers)*
Of Israel.

91

One, two, three,   *(close fingers—one at a time)*

Saul, David,   *(open one at a time)*

And Solomon;   *(open third finger)*

Crown all three.   *(place crown on head)*

I'LL WHISPER HIS NAME

God sent Him down   *(point finger up then down)*
To show God's love for us. *(point to self—then to class)*
What is His name?   *(whisper name)*
I'll whisper it for you.   *(put finger to mouth)*
   JESUS   *(whisper)*

TEN PEOPLE

Ten tall people   *(hold up ten fingers)*
People full of love.
See them bow their heads *(bend at knuckles)*
And pray to God above?

I PRAY

I fold my hands   *(fold for prayer)*
And bow my head   *(bow head)*
I pray to God
Beside my bed.   *(kneel down)*

I THANK GOD

I bounce my ball,   *(bounce ball)*
And play all the day.
At night I thank God   *(fold hands in prayer)*
For letting me play.

LITTLE SHEEP

Jesus is the Shepherd.   *(hold up index finger, right hand)*
I am just a little sheep;   *(hold up thumb, left hand)*
He is always near me—   *(bring finger close to thumb)*
When I'm awake or asleep.

ONLY ONE SHEPHERD

This is the shepherd,   *(hold up index finger—right hand)*
These are his sheep.   *(hold fingers of left hand down—*
                                slightly spread)
They follow him all the day;   *(move both hands to right)*
Another shepherd   *(hold up middle finger—right hand)*
May call to them   *(stop sheep to listen)*
But the sheep just turn away.   *(turn left hand around, move*
                                quickly away)

HIGH, HIGH, HIGH

We're little people,   *(put hand low)*
You and I.   *(point to child, then self)*
But our songs to God   *(hold palms upward)*
Rise high, high, high.   *(raise hands higher and higher)*

WHAT IS AN IDOL?

What is an idol?   *(spread hands in question)*
A god made with hands.   *(mold an object with both hands)*
It can't think,   *(touch head)*
It can't talk,   *(touch lips)*
It can't hear,   *(touch ear)*
It can't walk: *(walk two fingers)*
Nor hear a prayer.   *(hold hands out as if beseeching—*
                                straight in front)
It can only stare!   *(do not blink eyes)*

WHAT DO IDOLS LOOK LIKE?

What do idols look like?   *(spread hands—p*
Maybe fat,   *(reach out arms i*
Maybe thin;   *(make small circ*
Maybe short,   *(measure short h...*
Maybe tall;   *(measure high in air)*
Maybe sad,   *(pull corners of mouth down)*
Maybe glad;   *(pull corners of mouth up)*
That's what idols look like!

GOD MADE THE COLORS

God made
   The blue sky,   *(point up)*
   The green grass,   *(point down)*
   The white snow,   *(hold hands high; flutter*
             fingers downward)

   The yellow sun,   *(point up)*
   What handful of colors?   *(hold up cupped hand)*
   The rainbow.   *(extend arms outward at*
             sides—palms down)

LET'S MAKE A TREE

A little tree,   *(hold up one finger for tree)*
A bigger tree,   *(hold up arm, bent at elbow)*
A great big tree I see.   *(hold up arm, straight)*
Now let's count the trees
   we've made.
One, two, three.   *(make and count each tree again)*

THE JORDAN RIVER

Draw a crooked line   *(do so, vertically in the air)*
For the Jordan river.
To say it is short would be wrong;
For—stretched out like this—   *(stretch river out straight)*

.o zig-zags in it—
.wo hundred miles long!   *(look at it in amazement)*

WHAT IS THE CHURCH?

What is the church?   *(put finger to head in thought)*

A building with a steeple?   *(touch index fingers to make steeple)*

No, look inside—   *(open doors)*
There's the church: the people!   *(wiggle all fingers)*

THE LORD'S DAY

This child says, "It's a pretty day. Let's go out and play."	*(point to index finger—left hand)*
This child says, "This is the Lord's day, And we need to pray."	*(point to next finger)*
This child says, "Let's each bring someone Else along with us."	*(point to next finger)*
This child says, "We want our friends To learn about Jesus."	*(point to next finger)*
This child says, "We will number then, *Not just five*—but ten!"	*(point to thumb)* *(hold up five fingers—then, ten)*

HERE IS A BABY BIRD

Here is a baby bird, He is learning to fly. Now watch him get ready To take off to the sky!	*(flap wings slowly and awkwardly)* *(flap wings faster)* *(up on tiptoes)* *(jump softly)*

THE SEA OF GALILEE

The Sea of Galilee Looks like a pear. No matter where you sail, The fish are there.	*(point as a teacher)* *(arms shape like pear)* *(cup hands long wise for boat)* *(wiggle two hands for two fish)*

ONE OR MORE?

One finger alone cannot do much;   *(hold up index finger—right hand)*
Add four more to it—   *(open all fingers—right hand)*
What a clutch! See?   *(right hand clutch)*
One Christian alone cannot   *(hold up index finger left hand)*
  do much;
Add four more to him—   *(open all fingers—left hand)*
The church grows! See?   *(hold up and wiggle all ten
                                 fingers repeatedly)*

WHAT IS THIS?

Tell me! Tell me! What is this?   *(make rectangle with arms)*
It is a very big bus.   *(move bus along)*
It takes children every week   *(keep bus moving)*
To hear all about Jesus.

KNOCK, KNOCK!

My friend knocked, knocked   *(knock on door)*
At my house last week.
Together *we* went to the   *(walk two fingers away from you)*
  Lord's house.
This week we knocked, knocked   *(knock with both hands)*
At my neighbor's house.
And *we three* went to the   *(walk three fingers away from you)*
  Lord's house.

THE HAPPY WAY

To please God   *(point up)*
You can pray.   *(praying hands)*
Obey God—   *(point up)*
It's the happy way!   *(smile and nod head)*

TWO BROTHERS

This is Peter   *(hold up index finger)*
And Andrew his brother: *(hold up other index finger)*

Just look and see   *(hook two index fingers together)*
How they loved each other!   *(raise hooked fingers)*

THE LETTER T

T—is for Timothy   *(form the letter T)*
And for Titus
Both worked with Paul   *(hold up index fingers—side
                                        by side)*
Both preached "Jesus."   *(form a cross with two fingers)*

A PROPHET

A prophet told people   *(with left index finger, point to people)*
(1) What would happen *here today*   *(then point straight down)*
Or warned the people   *(point out with right index finger)*
(2) What would happen *far away.*   *(point far away)*

LET US MAKE A MOUNTAIN

Let us make a mountain   *(touch finger tips—hands
                                        spread apart some)*

This is the way.
Men often climb mountains   *(raise mountain slightly)*
To do this: Pray.   *(close hands to make praying
                                        hands)*

BABY JESUS GREW

Baby Jesus grew and grew   *(hold hands low; then
                                        shoulder high)*

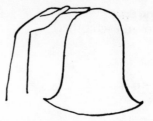

Till he was big as me
  and you.

(put hand on your head)

BABY PIG

Oink, oink! said baby pig,

*(speak softly; raise
  fist for pig)*

What shall I eat this morn?
Oink, oink, said mother pig—

*(speak louder; make
  fist larger)*

The tall yellow corn.

BABY SHEEP

Baa, baa, said baby sheep,

*(speak softly; tight
  fist for sheep)*

And what do I eat?
Baa, baa, said mother
  sheep —
The grass at your feet.

(speak louder; enlarge fist)

BE LIKE JESUS

I like to pray,
I like to give,
To hear the book God
  gave us.
I like to sing,
I like to help,
Then *I* shall be like *Jesus*.

(fold hands)
(drop money in plate)
(hand to ear)

(hold songbook)
(hold out hands)
*(point to self and to
  heaven)*

BIBLE HOUSES

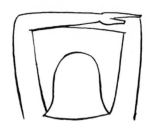

Houses in Bible times   *(make square with arms)*
Were square like *that*,   *(nod at square)*
Roofs of the houses then

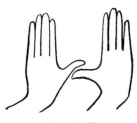

Looked like this—flat.   *(lay hands flat—*
                                   side by side)

THE BIRDS' UMBRELLAS

What do the birds do   *(flap arms)*
Up in the sky —   *(look up)*
For an umbrella   *(right hand flat above*
                                   index finger — left hand)

To keep them dry?
They fly to a tree   *(flap arms)*
That stands nearby,   *(one arm upright;*
                                   fingers spread)

And under its leaves,
They keep nice and dry.   *(nod)*

THE CAMEL

Some camels have *one* hump,   *(raise bent elbow)*
Some camels have *two* humps; *(raise both elbows)*

But they all live in the desert.
Desert sand is quite hot!   *(raise one foot as if burned)*
But camels *must* walk there.
So why do their feet never *(spread hands)*
 hurt?
Because God made camels   *(point skyward)*
With soft pads on their feet — *(point to feet)*
That's why camels' feet never
 hurt!

THE CAMEL'S HUMP

This is the big hump   *(cross bent arms)*
On the camel's back;
People sit on it
Just like a big sack.   *(make sack)*

THE CLOCK

One o'clock, two o'clock, *(two fingers in turn)*
Small though I be;
Three o'clock, four o'clock, *(alternate the fingers*
Jesus loves me.   *each time)*
Five o'clock, six o'clock,
When I'm not bad;
Seven o'clock, eight o'clock,
Jesus is glad.
Nine o'clock, ten o'clock,
I will not fear;
'Leven o'clock, twelve o'clock,
Jesus is near.

COUNT WITH ME

One, two — God loves you, *(count on fingers)*
Two, three — God loves me.
Three, four—and many
 more;
Four, five — everyone alive!

FIVE CHILDREN

This child said, "I hear a
   great shout!"
This child said,
   "What's it all about?"
This child said,
   "I see a lame man walk."
This child said,
   "I hear a dumb man talk!"
This child said,
   "Jesus is here, no doubt!"

*(hold up another finger
each time)*

FIVE LOST SHEEP

Five little sheep

Were walking one
   bright day;
They walked so far,
That they *all* lost their way!

Who found the lost sheep?
The shepherd, tall and slim.
He called each one—
Were they glad to see him!

*(hold fingers left hand
downward)*
(walk the fingers along)

(hold up right index finger)
(make sheep again)
*(move sheep quickly
to shepherd)*

GOD LOVES ALL CHILDREN

Some children are short,
Some children are tall;
Whether tall or short,
God loves them all.

(hand measures low)
(hand measures high)
(hand high; then low)
(arms wide)

GOD MAKES THE SUN SHINE

God makes the sun shine.
God makes the rain fall.
But not just for me.
It's for one and all.

(circle with arms)
(flutter fingers downward)
(point to self)
(point to others)

GOD SEES ME

Here is the big world,   (circle arms)
Big as it can be.
I'm just a little child,   (point to self)
But God can see me.   (look up; point to self)

GOD TAKES CARE OF ME

If God takes care of   (point to heaven)
Each bird we see,   (flap arms)
Won't he take care of
Both you and me?   (point to class; then, self)

THE HAPPY PEOPLE

The people run together,   (run fingers along arm)
There's not one frown;   (pull mouth into smile)
Why are they so happy?
Jesus is in town!   (clap hands softly)

HOW MANY HAVE YOU?

Four brothers Jesus had;   (four fingers of right hand)
And sisters? At least two.   (two fingers of left hand)
Say, how many brothers   (lower hands)
(And sisters, too) have you?   (point to different ones)

HOW MUCH DO I LOVE GOD?

How much do I love God?   (point to self)
An inch? Oh, no!   (measure inch)
That is not enough!   (shake head)
I love God—sooooo!   (arms wide)

I AM A FARMER

I am a farmer,   *(point to self)*
And my hoe is big.   *(hold hoe ready for use)*
Each day I take it
And dig, dig, dig.   *(do so three times)*

I HAVE TWO PENNIES

I have two pennies, God: *(hold out left hand*
One, two.   *(count into other hand)*
On Lord's day, I give both
To you.   *(drop in plate)*

I MUST DO GOOD

I must do good   *(point to self)*
Each day of the week,
If I want to go to heaven.   *(point up)*

How many days
Are there in a week?   *(hold fists up)*
One, two, three, four, five,   *(count off)*
        six, seven!

I PET MY DOG

I pet my dog   *(do so)*
For I find
Jesus wants *me*   *(point to self)*
To be kind.   *(pet dog again)*

I TAKE TWO SEEDS

I take two seeds,   *(extend open hands)*
I plant them—so.   *(close hands)*
What does God send?   *(look up)*
        Showers.

I look each day   *(look at closed hands)*
To see them grow.
What will come up?   *(raise index fingers slowly)*
        Flowers!

105

I TALK TO GOD

God talks to me in the Bible.	(open book)
I talk to God when I pray.	(folded hands)
God and I talk to each other	(nod)
At least three times every day.	(three fingers)

I WORSHIP GOD

I worship God	(raise arms in praise)
In the meeting-house;	(touch all fingertips for building)
I sit as quiet	
As a little mouse.	(whisper last line)

LET'S MAKE A FISH

Let's make a fish;	(palms together; weave hands back and forth)
A *bigger* fish!	(push one palm forward a *little*)
A great *big* fish — see?	(make *still* longer fish)
Now let us count	(hold up open left hand)
The fish we've made:	
One and two — and three!	(count)

LET'S MAKE A FISH NET

Let's make a fish net,	(palms up; fingers interlocked)
Now cast it in the sea.	(cast net)
Let's pull it back—so.	(pull back)
Is it full or empty?	(wiggle fingers for fish in net)

MEET JIMMY

Meet a certain little boy.   *(raise index finger)*
His name is Jimmy.
Can you guess why all
    his friends
Now call him *Gimmy?*   *(extend open hands; close*
                                 and jerk toward you)

MY HANDS

Right hand,   *(address right hand)*

Now left hand,   *(address left hand)*

Come together—do!   *(clasp hands)*
Jesus
Has much work

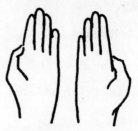

For you to do.   *(offer hands to heaven)*

OPEN THE GATES

See the walls of   *(make square with arms)*
　* Jerusalem?
And these are the gates   *(open and close hands)*
　so wide.
Open the gates wide   *(hands open)*
　each morning
Let the people come inside.

See the walls of   *(make square with arms)*
　Jerusalem?
And these are the gates   *(open and close hands)*
　so wide.
Shut all the gates in   *(close hands)*
　evening
Keep the people safe
　inside.

*Substitute other walled cities.

SEE THE FIVE FISHERMEN

See the five fishermen   *(lace fingers for boat;*
　　　　　　　　　　　　　　　wiggle five)

In their little boat?
Busy are they, fishing
While they float and float.   *(float boat along)*

SEE THE STAR?

See the star shining bright? *(hold up open hand)*
Make it twinkle in the night! *(wiggle fingers)*

SEE THE SUN?

See the sun in the sky? *(make circle with fingers)*
It will set by and by.   *(lower circle slowly)*

SEE THE TWO LITTLE LAMBS?

See the two little lambs —   *(two fists tight)*
    watch them grow!
They will be big sheep   *(big fists)*
    some day, you know.

SEVEN DAYS

There are seven days in   *(seven fingers)*
    each week.
Now which is called the   *(cock head)*
    Lord's day?
To find out, just close   *(close all but first finger)*
    these fingers —
The *first* day is the   *(raise finger)*
    Lord's day!

THE SHEEPFOLD

Here is a sheepfold—   *(make square with arms)*
Big and wide;
The shepherd keeps the   *(index finger — right hand)*
    sheep
Safe inside.   *(speak softly on last line)*

SWEETEST NAME

Five letters —   *(hold fingers – left hand)*
Just one word,
The sweetest name
Ever heard.   *(cup ear with other hand)*
    J-E-S-U-S!   *(point to each finger of*
        left hand)

TEN LITTLE CHILDREN

Ten little children,	*(hold up ten fingers)*
Living in one block;	
Five went to worship,	*(lower left hand)*
Five did not.	*(put left hand behind you)*
Then *this* five told that *five.*	*(raise right hand; then*
	left hand)
How they liked to go.	*(nod head)*
Now, all *ten* children	*(ten fingers)*
Worship in a row.	

WHAT AM I?

Sometimes I am big,	*(big circle with arms)*
Sometimes I am small;	*(small circle)*
You see me at night.	
I look like a ball!	
What am I?	
(THE MOON)	*(nod head)*
Sometimes I am big,	*(large circle with arms)*
Sometimes I am small;	*(small circle)*
Daytimes you see me.	
I look like a ball!	
What am I? (THE SUN)	*(nod head)*

WHAT CAN I DO?

One, two,	*(count as you go)*
What can I do?	
Three, four,	
To please God more?	
Five, six,	
My hair I fix,	
Seven, eight,	
So I'm not late,	
Nine, ten,	
Lord's day at 10:00!	

WHAT CAN I DO FOR THE SICK?

I am just a little child.	*(point to self)*
What can I do for the sick?	
I know what to do.	*(clap hands softly)*
It will please God too!	
I can give something to them	
All the flowers I can pick	*(pick some)*

WHAT DO I DO?

What do I do?	*(point to self)*
When I am sad?	
I think of Jesus—	*(look to heaven)*
Then I am glad.	*(raise arms to heaven and smile)*

WHO LOVES JESUS?

Who loves Jesus?	*(raise index fingers in turn)*
Who loves God?	
All who do—let your	*(nod)*
head nod.	
Who likes to sing?	*(make songbook; then pray)*
Who likes to pray?	
All who do—stretch up	*(stretch on tiptoes)*
this way!	

WHO WILL GO?

Who will go to Bible Study?	*(spread hands)*
I ask three friends one day.	*(three fingers)*
"I will,"	
"I will,"	
"I will," they say.	*(point to each friend)*
Now we four friends are	*(hook arms)*
on our way.	

WIND AND LISTEN

Wind and listen,   *(wind watch; hold to ear)*
Wind and listen,   *(repeat)*
I do this every day.
Each tick tells me   *(listen)*
That God loves me.   *(point to self)*
He loves *you* the same way!   *(point to others)*